D1582227

3 0116 02063183 2

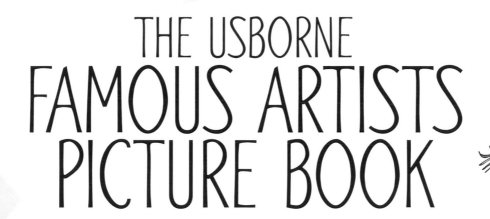

THE USBORNE
FAMOUS ARTISTS
PICTURE BOOK

Megan Cullis

Illustrated by Mark Beech

Designed by Nicola Butler

Edited by Rosie Dickins and Jane Chisholm

Expert advice by Janice Wailes-Parton

CONTENTS

USBORNE QUICKLINKS

This book tells the stories of 29 famous artists, whose work spans hundreds of years and a wide range of styles. To zoom in on examples of their work, take virtual tours of art galleries and find lots of art activities, go to the Usborne Quicklinks website at www.usborne.com/quicklinks and type in the keywords 'famous artists picture book'. Please read our internet safety guidelines at the Usborne Quicklinks website.

JAN VAN EYCK

Jan van Eyck was one of the first artists in Northern Europe to demonstrate the amazing effects of oil paints. He was so good, many people thought he invented them. His paintings have a glossy, jewel-like finish, which he achieved by building up lots of thin, transparent layers of oil paint.

Born in Maaseik, in what is now Belgium, little is known about van Eyck's early life. By the time he was in his twenties, he was a hugely successful painter, working for many rich, powerful clients. In 1425, he went to work for the Duke of Burgundy in the city of Bruges. A few years later, he was sent to Portugal to paint the Duke's future wife, Isabella of Portugal, in order to check her suitability as a bride.

Van Eyck died in 1441, leaving many unfinished paintings behind.

KEEPING IT IN THE FAMILY

Some people think Jan van Eyck had a brother, Hubert, and a sister, Margaret, who were artists too. Jan and Hubert were thought to have worked closely together – sometimes Hubert would start a painting leaving Jan to finish it.

Experts believe that the portait below is of van Eyck himself. The inscription at the bottom, in Latin, says, 'Jan van Eyck made me on 21 October 1433'.

PORTRAIT OF A MAN (SELF-PORTRAIT)
Painted in 1433

The portrait on the left shows van Eyck's wife, Margaret, wearing a horned headdress. Van Eyck may have painted it to hang next to his own portrait.

The painting below was paid for by a rich churchman named Rolin, shown on the left. Opposite him sit baby Jesus and his mother, Mary. Although it looks as if Rolin is in the same room, the other figures are supposed to be in a heavenly scene in his imagination.

THE VIRGIN AND CHILD WITH CHANCELLOR ROLIN
Painted between 1434-35

The tiny figure in the background wearing a red headdress may be a portrait of Van Eyck himself.

MARGARET, THE ARTIST'S WIFE
Painted in 1439

The painting on the right tells the story of the Angel Gabriel as he announces to the Virgin Mary that she will bear the son of God. The painting is full of luxurious textures, from the polished wood flooring, to the rich, velvety robes.

MINUTE DETAIL

Van Eyck's paintings contain such tiny details, many people think he used a magnifying glass to paint them.

ANNUNCIATION
Painted between 1434-36

PIETER BRUEGEL I

This drawing of an artist by Bruegel may be a self-portrait.

Born into a large family of painters, Pieter Bruegel is famous for creating lively, outdoor scenes.

He started painting and drawing in his home town of Antwerp, in what is now Belgium. Inspired by his surroundings, Bruegel often painted crowds of people at local festivals, dances and games.

In his late thirties, Bruegel moved to Brussels, where he built up an impressive reputation. The City Council even asked him to paint several pictures to celebrate the building of a new canal between Antwerp and Brussels.

Bruegel died at around the age of 44, leaving behind two sons, who later became artists themselves. He is often known as Pieter Bruegel the Elder, to distinguish him from his oldest son, Pieter.

HUNTERS IN THE SNOW (WINTER)
Painted in 1565
This painting illustrates the month of January. It shows two huntsmen trudging through the snow, leading their tired dogs home. Below them, townspeople skate on frozen ponds, having fun in the chilly weather.

The photograph below shows Brussels today. The town hall in the centre was built about 100 years before Bruegel was born.

The unsettling drawing below shows a man cutting open a monstrous fish's belly with a huge knife. Smaller fish are tumbling out of its mouth and body. Drawings like this one were so popular, they were later made into black-and-white prints.

Full of energy and life, this picture shows around 125 lively guests at an outdoor wedding. In the bottom right-hand corner, a musician plays a kind of bagpipe as cheerful guests dance around him.

BIG FISH EAT LITTLE FISH
Drawn using pen and ink in 1556

THE WEDDING DANCE
Painted in 1566

DRESSING UP
A story goes that Bruegel dressed up in workers' clothes so he could mingle in the crowds at weddings and fairs and find inspiration for his paintings.

LEONARDO DA VINCI

Leonardo is considered to be one of the greatest artists of all time. He excelled at anything he put his mind to, from science, maths and architecture, to thinking up incredible new inventions.

Born in the village of Vinci, Italy, he was sent to Florence when he was just 14 years old to study with a painter named Verrocchio. It's said Verrocchio was so impressed by his pupil that he vowed never to paint again.

Leonardo's astonishing skills soon caught the attention of the Duke of Milan, and in 1482, he became an official painter at the Duke's court. His work was so admired that in 1517 he was called to Rome to work for the Pope, leader of the Catholic Church, and later to France, to work for the French king.

Despite his many talents, Leonardo rarely finished what he started. Only around ten completed paintings survive today. He died in France in 1519, and stories say that the king held Leonardo in his arms during his final moments.

SELF-PORTRAIT AS AN OLD MAN
Painted in 1512

CHILDHOOD HOME

Leonardo da Vinci means 'Leonardo from Vinci'. The house he grew up in still stands in the hills just outside the village.

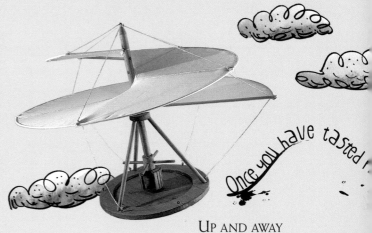

Once you have tasted

AMAZING INVENTIONS

Leonardo jotted down his inventions, including water mills, cranes and all kinds of flying machines, in notebooks like this.

UP AND AWAY

This is a model of one of Leonardo's flying machines. In fact, the design would have been too heavy to lift off the ground and fly.

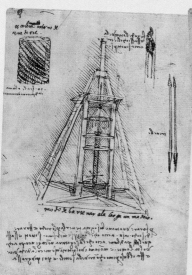

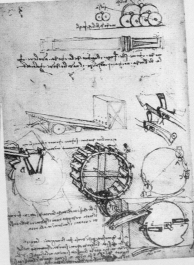

The noblest pleasure is the joy of understanding.

The writing is reversed and only reads properly when you look at it in a mirror. Leonardo may have done this to keep his notes secret.

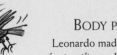

BODY PARTS

Leonardo made hundreds of scientific studies of bodies. He developed new ideas about how they worked, and hoped to publish his findings in a book, but he never got around to it.

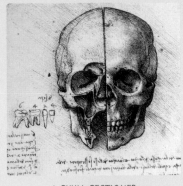

A SKULL SECTIONED
Drawn in 1489

This detailed drawing shows a human skull.

MONA LISA
Painted between 1503-06

Probably the most famous painting of all time is Leonardo's portrait, *Mona Lisa*. The woman in the portrait is Lisa Gherardini, an Italian merchant's wife. Her strange half-smile fascinates people, as it is so difficult to pin down.

ANIMAL LOVER

Leonardo loved animals and refused to eat meat. It's said he bought caged birds just to let them go.

This portrait shows Cecilia Gallerani – a young companion of the Duke of Milan – holding an animal called an ermine. Ermines were prized for their white coats, and were often used as a symbol of purity.

LADY WITH AN ERMINE
Painted in 1490

...u will forever walk the earth with your eyes turned skyward...

WAR

In 1499, war broke out in Italy. Leonardo was living in Milan at the time, but he had no trouble finding work elsewhere. He earned a living designing maps and weapons for powerful noblemen.

THE LAST SUPPER
Painted between 1495-97

Leonardo made this painting on a wall inside a monastery. It was hailed as a masterpiece, and took him three years to complete. Unfortunately, Leonardo experimented with the undercoat and the paint began flaking off almost as soon as he finished it.

One of the greatest sculptors of all time, Michelangelo also excelled in painting, architecture and poetry.

Born in a small village near Florence, Italy, he started out as a painter's apprentice at the age of 13. Word of his talent spread, and he began to take on work for wealthy art-lovers in Florence and Rome. He soon caught the eye of the Pope and was commissioned to paint the ceiling of the Sistine Chapel in the Vatican City, inside Rome.

During his 60s, Michelangelo worked as an architect, designing grand buildings in Florence and Rome. In 1547 he designed an enormous dome for St. Peter's church in Rome. Sadly, he died before building began, but the dome now stands as the tallest church dome in the world.

PORTRAIT OF MICHELANGELO
Painted in around 1535
The painting above of Michelangelo was made by one of his followers, Jacopino del Conte.

I saw the angel in the marble and carved until I set him free.

DAVID
Sculpted between 1501-04

This statue shows the biblical character David. Florentine officials asked Michelangelo to carve a statue out of a huge block of marble. It was such a challenge, the statue took two years to complete.

Michelangelo had to work at a back-breaking angle to paint the ceiling.

THE SISTINE CHAPEL CEILING
Painted between 1508-12
To paint this ceiling, Michelangelo applied paint to wet plaster – a technique known as *fresco*. The painting contains over 300 carefully arranged figures telling different stories from the Bible, and it took Michelangelo over four years to complete.

My brush is always above me; it drips and dribbles making a splendid mosaic on my face below!

RAPHAEL

Raphael was one of the most famous painters of his day. Born in Urbino, Italy, he learnt to paint from his father, an official painter for the Duke of Urbino. When his father died, Raphael took over the family workshop.

At 21, he moved to Florence, where he met and studied many artists, including Michelangelo and Leonardo da Vinci. Soon after, he was called to the Vatican City by the Pope to decorate various rooms in the Pope's palace.

Raphael was admired across Europe, and one critic even said his work was 'more lifelike than life itself'. He died from fever at the age of just 37.

SELF-PORTRAIT
Painted in 1506

This photograph shows Urbino,
where it's thought Raphael was born.

RIVALRY
Although Raphael and Michelangelo became great rivals,
Raphael was fascinated by Michelangelo's work. Many of Raphael's
paintings are inspired by Michelangelo's figures and compositions.

THE GARVAGH MADONNA
Painted between 1509-10

This is one of many paintings by Raphael
showing the baby Jesus with his mother, Mary,
and his cousin, St. John. The figures are arranged
in a pyramid to symbolize the strong
relationship between them.

What Raphael
knew of art he
learned from me.

Michelangelo was said to dislike
Raphael, and complained that
he copied his work.

THE SCHOOL OF ATHENS
Painted between 1510-12

Raphael painted this scene on the wall of the Pope's library in the Vatican. It shows some of the most famous thinkers of ancient times.

BABY ANGELS
Raphael is famous for drawing
and painting charming baby angels,
like this one. They are sometimes
known as cherubs, or *putti*.

TITIAN

Tiziano Vecellio, known as Titian, was one of the greatest Italian painters of the 16th century, renowned for his brilliant use of colour. His talent was so dazzling, a fellow painter described him as 'the Sun among small stars'.

At around the age of 10, Titian went to Venice, where he trained under two painters, Gentile and Giovanni Bellini. About twelve years later, he moved to Padua to work on a series of church wall paintings.

Titian became the official state painter of Venice in 1516, and went on to work for dukes, princes, the Pope and even Emperor Charles V, ruler of the Spanish Empire. In 1576, he died of a plague which swept through Venice. Thousands died, but he was so famous and well respected, he was the only one given a proper burial service.

SELF-PORTRAIT
Painted in about 1562-67
This self-portrait is of
Titian at about 70 years old.

VENICE
This map of Venice was painted in around 1620, and shows a busy, thriving city. During Titian's time, Venice was the wealthiest city in the world.

FUSSY ARTIST
Titian was such a perfectionist that he kept his pictures in his studio for up to ten years, going back to retouch them again and again.

Painting done under pressure... can only give rise to formlessness.

It is not bright colours but good drawing that make figures beautiful.

THE HOLY FAMILY WITH A SHEPHERD
Painted in about 1510
This painting shows the Virgin Mary with her son, Jesus, and her husband, Joseph. A shepherd kneels before the baby. Mary is bathed in a glow of light, directing the viewer's eye towards Jesus. Her shimmering, velvety cloak contrasts with the rugged landscape in the background.

PORTRAIT OF GEROLAMO (?) BARBARIGO
Painted in about 1510

This elegant and refined man was a member of an aristocratic Venetian family named Barbarigo. His enormous silvery-blue quilted sleeve is painted in amazing detail.

8

CARAVAGGIO

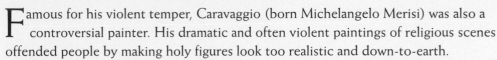

Famous for his violent temper, Caravaggio (born Michelangelo Merisi) was also a controversial painter. His dramatic and often violent paintings of religious scenes offended people by making holy figures look too realistic and down-to-earth.

Caravaggio started his career painting flowers and fruit to sell in the streets of Rome. His big break came in 1599, when he won the first of several important jobs making religious paintings to decorate churches. He soon became famous across Europe – as much for his unpredictable behaviour as for his talent. In 1606, he killed a man in a fight over a tennis match, and was forced to flee Rome.

Caravaggio died, probably from fever, at the age of 38. One critic described him as an 'evil genius', and his art was quickly forgotten. It was rediscovered over 250 years later when realistic paintings had come into fashion, and it became clear how influential Caravaggio had been to other artists of his time.

PORTRAIT OF CARAVAGGIO
Drawn by Ottavio Leoni in 1621
This drawing is the only known portrait of Caravaggio by another artist.

This painting of a basket of fruit is so lifelike, there's even a maggot hole in the apple. Caravaggio claimed he put as much effort into painting a vase of flowers as into painting people.

This photograph of Rome today includes many buildings unchanged since Caravaggio's time.

THE BASKET OF FRUIT
Painted between 1597-99

CAUSING TROUBLE
Caravaggio was said to swagger around Rome with a sword in his hand, starting fights wherever he went. He once threw a plate of hot artichokes at a waiter in a fit of rage.

KNIGHTHOOD
After leaving Rome, Caravaggio sailed to Malta, where he began painting for the Maltese Knights. He was made a knight in return, but was stripped of his honours when he started making trouble again.

SUPPER AT EMMAUS
Painted in 1601
This painting shows Jesus on the day he miraculously returned from the dead. Light falls dramatically across the painting, highlighting Jesus's face. The disciple on the right stretches his arms out theatrically, showing his surprise.

DIEGO VELÁZQUEZ

The official painter of the Spanish court, Diego Velázquez's realistic and truthful portraits made him a favourite of the Spanish king.

Velázquez grew up in Seville, Spain. At the age of 11, he began studying art with a local painter. Velázquez displayed exceptional talent and, in 1623, he was invited to Madrid to paint King Philip IV of Spain. A year later, he was made an official court painter to the king.

Rising up through the court, Velázquez eventually became Chamberlain to the Royal Household in charge of organizing ceremonies. In 1659, he was made a Knight of the Order of Santiago.

In 1660, Velázquez caught a fever and died. He is remembered as 'the painter's painter', and has become one of the most important figures in Spanish history.

Velázquez included this self-portrait in his painting, *The Maids of Honour*.

Before he moved to Madrid, Velázquez became popular for painting kitchen scenes showing ordinary people cooking, eating and drinking together. These kind of paintings were known as *bodegones*, which means 'taverns' in Spanish.

I would rather be the first painter of common things than second in higher art.

KITCHEN SCENE WITH THE SUPPER IN EMMAUS
Painted in 1651

ROYAL APPROVAL

King Philip was so enchanted by Velázquez's skill that he had a chair put in the artist's workshop so he could watch Velázquez paint at his leisure.

But the king refused to be painted as he grew older, as he didn't want a record of him looking aged.

THE MAIDS OF HONOUR
Painted in 1656

At the centre of this bustling scene is Philip IV's daughter, Margarita, surrounded by her attentive maids of honour and other courtiers. In the mirror on the wall, you can see a reflection of the king and queen.

On a visit to Rome, Velázquez painted the Pope, shown here on the left. The Pope was known for his violent temper, and Velázquez painted him with a stern expression. The portrait was so lifelike, the Pope apparently exclaimed, 'Too truthful!' when he saw it.

POPE INNOCENT X
Painted in 1650

FRANCISCO GOYA

Francisco Goya was the greatest Spanish artist of his time. He is famous for dreaming up gloomy, nightmarish scenes.

Born in a small village in Spain, Goya was apprenticed to a painter at 14. Four years later, he moved to Madrid. He began to make a name for himself painting portraits for wealthy patrons, and eventually caught the attention of the Spanish king. In 1789, he was made an official painter to the royal family.

In his late forties, Goya was struck by a terrible, unknown illness that nearly killed him, and left him deaf. He began to make horrifying pictures of strange, fantastical creatures. In the following years, war broke out in Spain, and Goya's pictures became even more disturbed.

In 1824, Goya moved to France, where he died at the age of 82.

SELF-PORTRAIT WITH GLASSES
Painted between 1797-1800

THE DUCHESS OF ALBA
Painted in 1797
Goya painted the Duchess of Alba several times, and the pair may have been linked romantically. In this portrait, the Duchess points to writing in the sand, which says *Solo Goya* – meaning 'Only Goya' in Spanish.

Goya often worked late at night, using candles on his hat to help him see.

In this frightening picture, Goya has imagined himself asleep on his desk, surrounded by ghostly owls and bats from his imagination. The writing in the picture says in Spanish, 'The sleep of reason produces monsters'.

Fantasy, abandoned by reason, produces impossible monsters.

THE SLEEP OF REASON PRODUCES MONSTERS
Printed in 1799

BLACK PAINTINGS
While he was ill, Goya moved to a house in the country where he covered the walls with dark scenes showing witches, warlocks and other evil creatures. The gruesome pictures became known as his 'black paintings'.

THE THIRD OF MAY, 1808 IN MADRID
Painted in 1814
This painting records some of the violence Goya witnessed when Spain was invaded by France during the war. The executioners are shown from behind as faceless killers, in contrast to the man in white, who stares wide-eyed ahead in terror.

11

REMBRANDT VAN RIJN

A miller's son from Leiden, Rembrandt van Rijn was the most successful Dutch artist of his time, famed for making portraits full of expression and life.

Rembrandt began his studies at Latin school, but at the age of 14 he abandoned his lessons to become an artist. In 1631, he moved to Amsterdam where he fell in love with Saskia, the daughter of a successful art dealer. The couple married just as Rembrandt's career took off, and Rembrandt began to make lots of money painting potraits for wealthy families and organizations.

Sadly, Saskia died in 1641, after giving birth to their only surviving child, Titus. Soon after, Amsterdam was hit by a financial crash, and Rembrandt declared himself bankrupt. He lived in poverty until his death in 1669.

SELF-PORTRAIT AS A YOUNG MAN
Painted in 1634
Rembrandt made over
90 self-portraits.

SELF-PORTRAITS

Rembrandt's self-portraits became so recognizable in Amsterdam, he became a celebrity. But he refused to flatter himself, and always painted his face with great honesty.

He often drew himself pulling faces to practise portraying different emotions.

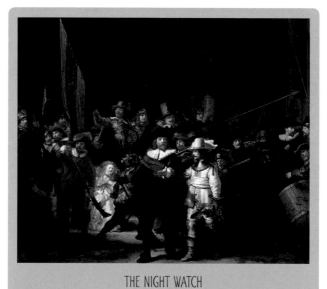

THE NIGHT WATCH
Painted in 1642
This painting is so big, the figures are almost lifesize.
The soldiers are dramatically lit against a dark background, and look as if they are about to march into action.

This grand house in Amsterdam was once owned by Rembrandt, but he was forced to sell it in the 1650s to pay his debts.

The house is now a museum containing many of his works.

BITS AND BOBS

Rembrandt filled his house with all kinds of exotic objects, from Roman busts, costumes and weapons to stuffed birds.

Rembrandt was superb at drawing, and sketched anything that interested him. He captured the rough, wrinkled skin of this elephant using lots of small lines.

AN ELEPHANT, A DRAWING
Drawn in about 1637

JAN VERMEER

Jan Vermeer is one of the most famous artists in the world, and yet little is known about his life. Almost all of his paintings are set in two rooms in his house in Delft, in the Netherlands.

Vermeer took over his father's business as an art dealer at the age of 20. At the same time, he began to paint, setting up lots of props and assistants in costume to create detailed scenes in his studio. Many of his paintings capture the bright light that flooded in from his studio's windows, but not the view outside.

Vermeer worked very slowly, and made little money from his art. His work was forgotten after his death, but his talents were rediscovered two centuries later, although only around 35 paintings of his survive today.

The figure on the left from one of Vermeer's paintings may have been a self-portrait. No other portrait of the artist exists.

HOME SWEET HOME

This peaceful scene is Vermeer's home city of Delft, and is his only known landscape. With its overcast sky, the viewer's eyes are drawn deep into the picture towards the light scattered over the rooftops at the back.

VIEW OF DELFT
Painted between 1660-61

BRILLIANT BLUE

In many of his paintings, Vermeer used lapis lazuli – an extremely expensive blue colour made from a type of semi-precious stone.

Vermeer ground up chunks of lapis lazuli into a fine powder. It was then carefully washed and mixed with a special type of oil to make the paint.

THE ARTIST'S STUDIO
Painted between 1665-66

The picture above was Vermeer's favourite painting, and he refused to sell it. It shows an artist at work in his studio, painting a woman dressed as Clio – a figure from Greek myth. She wears a wreath around her head and holds a trumpet and history book – three items connected with Clio.

LIFE IN DELFT

Vermeer led a busy life in Delft, working as an inn keeper and taking care of the family art-dealing business. This left little time to paint, and he only ever made around 60 paintings.

This photograph shows the street in Delft where Vermeer used to live and work.

JOHN CONSTABLE

A country boy from Suffolk, John Constable is celebrated for his vibrant English landscape paintings.

As a boy, he enjoyed regular sketching trips around the countryside. As soon as he was old enough, he moved to London to study art. But he became homesick for the country and returned to Suffolk every summer to paint.

Constable painted pictures of what he loved most – ordinary country life. Sadly, landscape painting was unfashionable at the time, and he failed to get the recognition he desired. Only towards the end of his life was he elected an academician of the Royal Academy of Arts – a highly respected school of art in London, led by the most prominent artists of its day. Finally, his talent was acknowledged.

PORTRAIT OF
JOHN CONSTABLE
AGED 20
By Daniel Gardner

Constable was a handsome man and had many admirers. One friend described him as 'like one of the young figures in the works of Raphael'.

PAINTING THE SKIES

Many of Constable's paintings are framed with spectacular rainbows, which he called 'this most beautiful phenomenon of light'.

Fascinated by cloudy skies, Constable sketched them wherever he went. He noted the exact time and location on the back of each study.

The sky is the keynote... the chief organ of sentiment... the sky is the source of light...

MARRIAGE

In his thirties, Constable fell in love with Maria Bicknell, a lawyer's daughter. However, her family considered him too poor, and he had to wait seven years until he could afford to marry her.

MARIA BICKNELL,
MRS JOHN CONSTABLE
Painted in 1816

THE HAY WAIN

Painted in 1821
Constable's most famous painting shows two men driving a horse-drawn cart – known as a 'wain' – across a shallow stream in Suffolk. In the distance, a group of farm labourers are cutting down hay, ready to fill the cart.

SIX-FOOTERS

Constable's largest paintings are known as his 'six-footers'. Before he began to paint, he made smaller watercolour sketches outside, before repainting the scene back in his studio using oils. One critic described his landscapes as the 'mirror of nature'.

14

J.M.W. TURNER

1775-1851

Born in London to a working-class family, Joseph Mallord William Turner grew up to be the most famous painter in England, known for his dramatic landscapes and wild seascapes.

Turner's childhood was spent sketching people in the busy London streets. His father, a barber, sold the drawings in his shop. At 14, Turner became a student at the Royal Academy. He soon became a huge success, and by the time he was 30, he had opened his own gallery to show his paintings. His bold, energetic style drew many critics, but their scathing comments only earned him more fame.

When he died in 1851, Turner left his collection to the nation. Most of his works are now on display at Tate Britain, London.

SELF-PORTRAIT
Painted in 1799
This self-portrait shows Turner at 24 years old. He stares out confidently at the viewer.

STORMY WEATHER
As he grew older, Turner developed a reputation for eccentricity. One story describes how he tied himself to a ship's mast to experience the drama of a storm at sea.

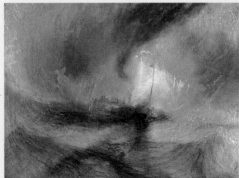

Bursting with energy, this painting shows a steam-boat in a storm. It shocked the public with its lack of detail – one critic even described it as 'soapsuds and whitewash'.

SNOW STORM: STEAM-BOAT OFF A HARBOUR'S MOUTH
Painted in 1842

THUMBS UP
Turner made scratchy marks in his paintings with his long, sharp thumbnail. He was said to have grown it so long it looked like an eagle claw.

Known as the 'painter of light', Turner filled his sketchbooks with paintings of light-filled skies – like this glowing sunset.

THE 'FIGHTING TEMERAIRE'
Painted in 1839
Turner was very fond of this painting, and called it his 'darling'. It shows a modern tug towing away a sailing ship for scrap. At the time, steam power was beginning to replace sails. The picture is said to be Britain's favourite painting.

Turner kept hundreds of different sketchbooks, which he carefully numbered and organized in his studio.

ÉDOUARD MANET

Photograph of Manet at the age of about 38

É douard Manet was one of the most original artists of the 19th century. His sketchy scenes of modern city life were unlike anything that had been seen before, and they created scandal and outrage.

Manet grew up in a wealthy household in Paris. All he wanted to do was paint, but his father encouraged him to follow more 'serious' pursuits. He was only allowed to study art after twice failing the entry exams to join the navy.

As a young painter, Manet was desperate to be accepted by the *Salon*, the official art exhibition in Paris. But many people were shocked by his work, and it wasn't until the late 1870s that critics finally began to appreciate his style. In 1881, he received one of the highest awards in France, the *Légion d'Honneur*. Manet said it came 'twenty years too late', and he died two years later.

The picture below shows a crowd of Parisians gathered to listen to an open-air concert. Manet used quick, broken brushstrokes to capture the excited mood of the crowd. Many critics dismissed the painting as looking rough and unfinished.

This photograph shows a fashionable area of Paris during Manet's day.

One must be of one's time, and paint what one sees.

MUSIC IN TUILERIES GARDENS
Painted in 1862
Manet included several of his friends and family in this painting, as well as a self-portrait on the far left.

Manet became great friends with the painter Berthe Morisot, whose portrait is shown here. Morisot encouraged Manet to paint out in the open air, in order to capture the changing effects of sunlight.

A skilled printmaker, Manet designed a print of two alley cats, shown in the middle of this poster. It was used to advertise a book by his famous writer friend, Champfleury.

BERTHE MORISOT WITH A BOUQUET OF VIOLETS
Painted in 1872

Insults are pouring down on me as thick as hail.

THE CATS' RENDEZVOUS

Printed in 1868

SCANDAL
Some of Manet's paintings horrified the public. *Olympia*, a painting of a naked woman looking boldly at the viewer, was described by one critic as 'neither true nor living nor beautiful'.

CLAUDE MONET

1840-1926

Monet is one of the world's most popular artists, famous for capturing the fleeting effects of nature in a loose, sketchy style known as Impressionism.

The son of a grocer, Monet grew up in the French port of Le Havre. Instead of concentrating on lessons at school, he filled his books with funny caricatures of his teachers. His father wanted him to take up the family grocery business, but Monet insisted on moving to Paris to study art. There, he met other young artists, including Édouard Manet and Pierre-Auguste Renoir, and began to develop a passion for painting outdoors.

At first, people made fun of Monet's style. By the 1880s, his exhibitions were a huge hit, and critics labelled him 'a poet of nature'. Monet moved to Giverny, a small village near Paris, and died a successful artist at the age of 86.

As he grew older,
Monet suffered eye problems.
He had to wear tinted glasses and
have an operation on his eyes.

As a young man, Monet earned extra money by selling caricatures. The sketch below shows his friend's head on the body of a butterfly.

CARICATURE OF JULES DIDIER
Drawn in 1860

Monet in his garden at Giverny

GARDEN AT GIVERNY

Monet bought a house in Giverny after admiring the pretty village from a train window. The house had a huge garden, where he created an exotic haven of weeping willows, bamboo and water lilies. He said, 'My garden is my most beautiful masterpiece.'

BRAVING THE ELEMENTS
To paint outdoors, Monet braved wind, rain and even snow. He wrapped himself in blankets and clutched a hot-water bottle to keep himself warm.

WATER LILIES: MORNING
Painted between 1914-15
Monet painted his water garden at Giverny hundreds of times. In this painting, the white water lilies and purple reflections on the water seem to dissolve into one endless wall of colour.

The picture on the left is just one section of a series of paintings designed to be viewed together. It was so big, it stretched from wall to wall in Monet's studio. Monet painted the water lilies so frequently, he claimed that his pond was enchanted.

Monet in his studio in 1920

EDGAR DEGAS

SELF-PORTRAIT
Painted between
1855-56

Degas painted this self-portrait
when he was 21. A shy, serious man,
he devoted all of his life to art.

Edgar Degas is famous as a painter of dancers. Born in Paris, he enrolled at law school at the age of 19. But he paid more attention to sketching in museums and, two years later, he switched to study art.

In 1870, war broke out, and Degas abandoned his art to join the French army. Soon after he returned from war, his father died, and his family fell into great debt. For the first time in his life, Degas had to make a living from his art, and was forced to sell his home. He began to help organize exhibitions with a group of artists, including Monet, and his paintings started to sell.

As he grew older, Degas shut himself away in his studio, obsessed by his work. His eyesight began to fail, but he stubbornly continued to sculpt and paint until he died in 1917.

THE DANCING LESSON
Painted in 1880
The painting above shows a group of young ballerinas stretching in a large rehearsal room,
while others rest at the side. Degas loved to create unusual, behind-the-scenes views.

LITTLE DANCER AGED 14
Drawn to the energy and grace of dancers, Degas spent many hours drawing ballerinas at the Paris Opera House.

This sculpture is dressed in real clothes. The effect is so lifelike, it frightened people when it was first exhibited.

Originally made out of wax between 1880-81, but cast in bronze in 1922, as shown here

I really wish to capture movement itself

PASTELS
This is Degas's box of pastels, showing the rich blues and purples he often used to sketch his dancers.

DANCER ADJUSTING HER SHOULDER STRAP
Photographed in 1895
In the 1880s, Degas began to dabble in photography – a new invention of the time. Although the dancer on the right looks as though she's turning around, she was posing very still.

VINCENT VAN GOGH

Despite only selling one picture in his lifetime, van Gogh's works now hang in galleries all around the world.

Born in the Netherlands, van Gogh began painting late, at the age of 27. He moved to Paris to stay with his brother, Theo, where he met a group of artists, including Paul Gauguin (see page 20). He soon became heavily influenced by their colourful, expressive styles.

After two years, Van Gogh left Paris for Arles, in southern France, looking for bright sunshine and light. He became desperately unhappy, and in 1889, admitted himself to a mental hospital. Over the next year, he painted feverishly. But at the age of 37, overcome with depression, he shot himself in the chest.

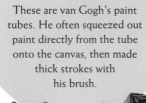

These are van Gogh's paint tubes. He often squeezed out paint directly from the tube onto the canvas, then made thick strokes with his brush.

SELF-PORTRAIT WITH A STRAW HAT
Painted in 1887

Painted in bright, sunny yellows and blues, van Gogh painted this vivid self-portrait soon after he began experimenting with colour.

SELF-PORTRAIT WITH A BANDAGED EAR
Painted in 1889

Van Gogh painted this self-portrait after a fierce argument with Gauguin. His ear is bandaged because he chopped part of it off.

SUNFLOWERS

Van Gogh lived near fields of bright sunflowers in Arles. He painted several pictures of them, and planned to decorate his friend Gauguin's room with the paintings when he came to stay.

LETTERS

Over the years, van Gogh wrote over 750 letters to his brother, Theo, telling him about his work. The brothers were very close, and Theo was a source of great comfort to van Gogh throughout his life.

Many of his letters are filled with sketches, which he called his 'scratches'.

STARRY NIGHT
Painted in 1889

This swirling landscape shows the night sky outside van Gogh's window at the mental hospital. He invented part of the village below.

PAUL GAUGUIN

Photograph taken in 1891

Born with a restless spirit, French artist Paul Gauguin spent his life dreaming of exotic, faraway lands. His early childhood was spent in Peru, but his family moved to Paris when he was seven. After a short time serving in the navy, he secured a job as a stockbroker, and then married.

Gauguin grew dissatisfied with his life. In 1883, he left his job, and later abandoned his family to become an artist. Over the next few years, he moved from place to place, searching for inspiration. In 1891, he set sail for Tahiti, in the South Pacific, where he produced his most famous paintings.

Struggling with debt and poor health, Gauguin moved to the Marquesas Islands in the Pacific in 1901, where he died two years later.

Gauguin spent several months in Brittany, where he painted *The Vision after the Sermon*. It shows a group of peasant women dressed in regional costume. They have just listened to a story from the Bible about a man who wrestled with an angel, and are imagining a vision of the story before them.

THE VISION AFTER THE SERMON
Painted in 1888

DRESSING UP
Gauguin was an eccentric character. He described himself as a 'noble savage', and during his stay in Brittany, began to dress in peasant clothes.

AREAREA
Painted in 1892
Gauguin used vivid colours to create this Tahitian landscape. In the background, three women dance around a giant statue of a moon goddess. Gauguin probably dreamt up this scene, inspired by local stories and Tahitian myths.

SKETCHES IN TAHITI
This is one of the sketchbooks Gauguin kept in Tahiti. He often used his sketches as the starting points for his paintings.

Gauguin used local materials to experiment with new techniques. Many of his Tahitian scenes were painted on old sacks, and he even carved sculptures out of coconuts, like the coconut face on the left.

HENRI MATISSE

1869-1954

Henri Matisse was one of the most influential artists of the 20th century. He initially trained as a lawyer, but at 20 he developed appendicitis and took up painting as he recovered in bed. Excited by his new hobby, he gave up law to become an artist.

For the next decade, Matisse was penniless. After stuggling for years, he exhibited his paintings in Paris in 1905 and finally made a breakthrough. Although some critics found his colourful style 'loathsome', the artist quickly rose to fame.

From around 1917, Matisse began to spend time in the south of France, and eventually settled there permanently. Although he suffered ill health in later life, he continued to work, until he died at the age of 84.

This photo shows Matisse in 1947 working inside his studio.

SUNSHINE IN THE SOUTH

In 1905, Matisse spent the summer in Collioure, a small fishing town in the south of France. He was delighted by the dazzling sunshine and bright colours of the sea and the sky.

VIEW OF COLLIOURE
Painted in 1905

Matisse painted the picture on the left while he was staying in Collioure. He began to experiment with a bold new style, and used strong brushstrokes to capture sunlight pouring across the rooftops.

When I started to paint, I felt transported into a kind of paradise...

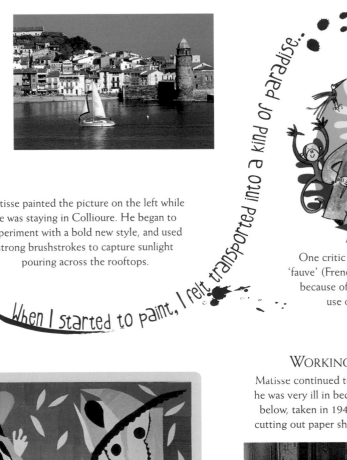

One critic called Matisse a 'fauve' (French for 'wild beast') because of his wild, exotic use of colours.

SORROW OF THE KING

Created in 1952
Many of Matisse's later pictures were made by cutting shapes out of paper, which he called 'drawing with scissors'. This vibrant example shows a king holding a guitar. A musician sits at his feet and a woman dances before them.

WORKING IN BED

Matisse continued to work even when he was very ill in bed. The photograph below, taken in 1949, shows Matisse cutting out paper shapes with scissors.

PABLO PICASSO

Pablo Picasso is probably the most famous artist of modern times. The son of an art teacher, he was born in southern Spain. According to his mother, baby Pablo started drawing before he could talk.

After studying in Spain, Picasso moved to Paris, the centre of the art world at the time. There, he began to experiment with a huge range of styles and materials, from soft, delicate pastels to bold paintings, sculptures, pottery and theatre designs.

In 1909, Picasso began working closely with an artist named Georges Braque. They made pictures that broke things down into shapes and showed them from different viewpoints. This style became known as Cubism.

Picasso moved to the south of France in 1946, soon after the Second World War. He died at the age of 92, leaving behind around 50,000 works of art.

PICASSO'S BREADROLLS
Photograph taken in 1952

This photograph, taken by French artist Robert Doisneau, shows Picasso's silly sense of humour – he's posing with loaves of bread for hands.

All children are artists. The problem is how to remain an artist once you grow up.

23-WORD NAME

Pablo's full name was 'Pablo Diego José Francisco de Paula Juan Nepomuceno María de los Remedios Cipriano de la Santísima Trinidad Martyr Patricio Clito Ruíz y Picasso'. He was named after various saints and relatives, but chose the single name 'Picasso' because he liked the way it sounded.

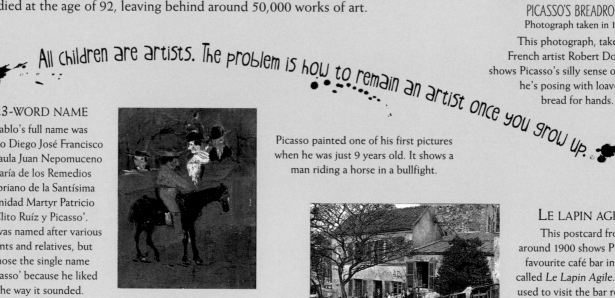

LE PICADOR
Painted in 1890

Picasso painted one of his first pictures when he was just 9 years old. It shows a man riding a horse in a bullfight.

LE LAPIN AGILE

This postcard from around 1900 shows Picasso's favourite café bar in Paris, called *Le Lapin Agile*. Picasso used to visit the bar regularly with other artists who lived in the area.

SEATED WOMAN (MARIE-THÉRÈSE WALTER)
Painted in 1937

This portrait shows Picasso's young girlfriend, Marie-Thérèse. Picasso painted her face and body from several different angles to draw attention to her most beautiful features, such as her almond-shaped eyes and elegant fingers. Picasso said, 'I paint what I know, not what I see.'

Picasso's studio in the south of France was next to a potter's scrapyard. The goat sculpture below is made from the scrap metal, wicker and pottery that Picasso found there.

Picasso had a pet goat, called Esmeralda, which he kept in his back yard along with this sculpture.

SHE-GOAT
Made in 1950

GEORGES BRAQUE

1882-1963

A French painter and sculptor, Georges Braque is famous as one of the creators of Cubism, and was a great friend of Picasso's.

Born in Paris, Braque's family moved to Normandy in Northern France when he was a young boy. He initially trained as a painter-decorator, but at the age of 18, he moved back to Paris and attended evening classes in drawing and painting. He began to paint bright, colourful landscapes, which he exhibited in his first art show in 1906.

A year later, Braque met Picasso. The pair soon began to meet every day to discuss their work, and together they invented Cubism.

In later life, Braque returned to Normandy, after serving in the French army during the First World War. He remained there until he died in 1963.

Portrait in the artist's studio, taken in around 1912

The strange-looking landscape on the right shows a dense group of trees arching over some houses below. Braque simplified what he saw into sharp angles and lines.

GREAT FRIENDS
Braque and Picasso worked so closely together, many of their paintings became almost impossible to tell apart. Braque said...

...It was like being roped together on a mountain.

TREES AT L'ESTAQUE
Painted in 1908

MUSICAL FORMS
Made in 1918
Together, Braque and Picasso invented a technique called collage. It involved cutting up bits of material and gluing them onto paper or canvas. The collage above is made from paper and card, cut into the shapes of different musical instruments. Can you see the outline of a guitar and a stringed guitar neck?

TREE OF JESSE
Designed in 1954
Braque designed this stained-glass window for his local church, using brilliant blues and turquoise. It shows a tree from the Bible, which has been simplified into angular shapes.

We must not imitate that which we seek to create.

Magritte often dressed like a businessman, in a dark suit and a bowler hat. Many of his paintings show ordinary men in bowler hats and suits.

Belgian artist René Magritte was a quiet, ordinary-looking man, with an extraordinary imagination. His paintings often show familiar objects in strange, impossible scenes.

Magritte had a troubled childhood. His mother killed herself when he was just 13. At 17, Magritte began to study art. Over the next few years, he painted while working part-time as a wallpaper and advertisement designer.

In 1927, Magritte moved to Paris, where he began to work with an exciting group of artists. Known as the Surrealists, they thought dreams could be more real than everyday life. But Magritte yearned for his native home, and returned to Brussels in 1930. He continued to make strange and mysterious pictures until his death in 1967, at the age of 68.

Magritte liked to say of the painting, 'Of course it's not a pipe! Just try putting tobacco in it!'

Ceci n'est pas une pipe.

THE TREACHERY OF IMAGES
Painted in 1929

The writing in the painting on the left reads, 'This is not a pipe.' in French. Magritte wanted to point out that paintings are only illusions, however real they look.

MAKING MONEY
At the end of the Second World War, Magritte was struggling to support himself. Some people say he and his brother forged banknotes to make money.

Art evokes the mystery without which the world would not exist.

HOME SWEET HOME
Magritte never worked in a studio, but preferred to paint in his kitchen or his dining room at home. He even wore a suit as he worked.

EMPIRE OF LIGHTS
Painted in 1952
This painting shows a dark, lamp-lit street against a bright, powder-blue sky. The impossible scene combines the elements of day and night, and creates a feeling of uneasiness.

Magritte painted four different versions of this scene. He said, 'In the world night always exists at the same time as day... But such ideas are not poetic. What is poetic is the visible image of the picture.'

SALVADOR DALÍ

Salvador Dalí was an eccentric man. Tall, slim, with a long, curly moustache, his theatrical personality became almost as famous as his art.

Born in Figueres, Spain, Dalí's childhood was marked by tragedy. His mother suffered from depression and died of cancer when Dalí was 16. In 1921, he moved to Madrid to study art, but he quickly found that he didn't fit in.

Dalí abandoned his studies and moved to Paris at 25, where he met the Surrealists. He felt instantly at home, and started making dream-like paintings, which he called 'hand-painted dream photographs'. He said they were accurate images of what he saw inside his head. Dalí became the most famous Surrealist artist, and a museum opened in 1974 in Figueres, Spain, devoted to his work. He died in Spain at the age of 85.

This photograph shows Dalí (on the left) with his painter friend, Georges Mathieu, at the Planetarium in London.

THE PERSISTENCE OF MEMORY
Painted in 1931

Dalí dreamed up the idea for the melting watches in this painting after he saw a round Camembert cheese melting in the sun. The orange clock in the bottom corner is covered in swarming ants, which Dalí used to represent decay.

BIG IMPRESSIONS

Dalí always liked to make an impact. In 1936, he gave a lecture about his art dressed in a deep-sea diving suit and helmet. Unfortunately, he had to be rescued when the helmet got stuck.

I just wanted to show that I was 'plunging deeply' into the human mind.

SPANISH HOME

Dalí often used Cadaqués – a town in Spain near his home – as inspiration for his work. You can see a similar landscape in his painting, *The Persistence of Memory*, above.

LOBSTER TELEPHONE
Made in 1936

The strange sculpture on the right combines two objects that you wouldn't expect to see together – a lobster and a telephone. Dalí once wrote, 'I do not understand why, when I ask for a grilled lobster in a restaurant, I am never served a cooked telephone.'

Lobster Telephone is made up of an ordinary, working phone, and a lobster sculpted out of plaster. Dalí produced five different versions of this sculpture, which are now on display in galleries around the world.

EDWARD HOPPER

A quiet, private man, Edward Hopper found fame painting empty landscapes and lonely scenes of city life. His moody, dramatically lit paintings were influenced by his love of films and plays.

Hopper began his career working as an illustrator in New York, designing covers for magazines and posters for advertising agencies. He grew to dislike his work, and began experimenting with his own style of painting in his spare time.

At 41, Hopper married a painter called Josephine Nivison. Around the same time, he held an exhibition of his watercolours, and it was an instant success. Hopper gave up his job and devoted himself to painting. By the time he died, Hopper's pictures were hanging in museums all over the United States.

This photograph shows Hopper in his studio in 1963.

BUG SURPRISE
Once, while he was at art school, he tricked a fellow student by painting bed bugs on paper, cutting them out and leaving them on his pillow.

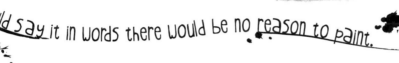
If you could say it in words there would be no reason to paint.

Many of Hopper's paintings show people alone in public spaces. The woman in this painting sits in an empty restaurant at night. The white shapes above her are the reflections of lights in the window. As she gazes into her coffee cup, she seems distracted and thoughtful.

AUTOMAT
Painted in 1927

Hopper's wife, Jo, served as the model for Automat. He adjusted her face to make her look younger, as she was 44 at the time.

KEEPING RECORDS
Hopper and his wife kept detailed records of all the pictures he exhibited and sold. This page records one such picture, with a sketch by Hopper and notes by his wife.

EARLY SUNDAY MORNING
Painted in 1930
The painting on the right may have been inspired by the New York street below. The shopfronts stretch out in a continuous line below a flat, blue sky. There is nobody around, only a fire hydrant and a barber's pole. The street feels strangely and eerily deserted.

FRIDA KAHLO

Frida Kahlo in 1944,
holding her pet monkey

Mexican painter Frida Kahlo caused a sensation with her striking, emotionally charged self-portraits. She was inspired by the bright colours and shapes of Mexican folk art.

Born in Coyoacán, Mexico, Kahlo contracted polio at the age of six. Twelve years later, she was seriously injured in a bus crash, and left with a broken spine. Traumatized by the accident, Kahlo suffered from severe pain for the rest of her life.

Kahlo abandoned her plans to become a doctor, and took up painting. She used art to express her feelings of pain and sadness. Before long, she caught the attention of a famous Mexican painter named Diego Rivera, and the couple married in 1929.

Kahlo died at just 47. Days before her death, she wrote, 'I hope the exit is joyful – and I hope never to return – Frida'.

Kahlo painted the picture below four years after her accident. It shows her last moments on board the bus before it crashed. Kahlo sits on the far right, wearing a red scarf. The workman, in blue overalls, later helped Kahlo as she lay injured on the street.

THE BUS
Painted in 1929

SELF-PORTRAIT (THE FRAME)
Painted in 1938
This is one of Kahlo's 55 self-portraits. She has painted herself wearing traditional Mexican dress, with ribbons and flowers in her hair. The decorative painted frame is inspired by Mexican folk art.

PLASTER ART
Kahlo spent much of her life wearing plaster casts, confined to her bed. She often decorated her plaster casts with pictures, turning them into art.

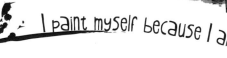

I paint myself because I am so often alone and because I am the subject I know best.

TROUBLED MARRIAGE
This photo shows Kahlo and husband, Rivera, in 1933. The couple had a troubled relationship, which Kahlo often expressed in her paintings.

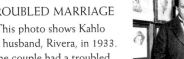

THE BLUE HOUSE
Kahlo was born in this blue house in Coyoacán and lived and worked there all her life. It is now a museum of her work. Her ashes are kept inside her bedroom in a funeral urn.

HENRY MOORE

A miner's son from Yorkshire, England, Henry Moore is one of the most famous sculptors of the 20th century. His bronze, wood and stone sculptures, inspired by nature, are on display all around the world, from Moscow to Milan.

Moore began sculpting at school and went on to study at Leeds School of Art. He was so talented that, in 1921, he was awarded a scholarship to study at the Royal College of Art – a well-known art school in London.

After finishing his studies, Moore began to take on public commissions and steadily built up a reputation worldwide. In 1929, he married a painter called Irina Radetsky, and the couple went on to have a daughter, Mary.

Moore died in 1986, leaving most of his money to a charity which he set up to encourage people to appreciate art.

This photograph shows Moore in his studio with his daughter Mary, in 1949.

YORKSHIRE HOME

This photograph, taken in around 1900, shows Castleford, the mining town in Yorkshire where Moore grew up.

MASK
Made in 1927

MASKS

Moore was fascinated by art from around the world, and visited museums regularly. He made this green stone mask, probably inspired by African masks.

Moore was interested in how different cultures interpreted human faces, and built up a collection of African and Mexican masks at home.

All art should have a certain mystery and should make demands on the spectator.

RAILWAY STATION DRAWINGS

During the Second World War, Moore was given a job as a war artist by the British government. He made lots of drawings of people sheltering from bombs in railway underground stations.

Afraid of disturbing people's sleep, Moore only made quick sketches on the station platforms before finishing the drawings back in his studio.

RECLINING FIGURE
Made in 1951
This sculpture was commissioned for the Festival of Britain – a national exhibition held after the war. It shows a female figure leaning back. Moore has simplified the woman's body into smooth, flowing lines and hollow spaces.

BARBARA HEPWORTH

1903-1975

English sculptor Barbara Hepworth became famous for her flowing sculptures made out of wood, stone and bronze. She was one of the first female sculptors to carve her own work into wood or stone – before her, artists usually modelled in clay or plaster first, and had the model carved by a craftsman.

Born in Yorkshire, Hepworth studied at Leeds School of Art, where she became great friends with the sculptor Henry Moore. Like him, in 1921, she won a scholarship to the Royal College of Art in London.

In 1939, Hepworth moved to Cornwall with her children, just before the Second World War broke out. Her reputation as a sculptor soared after taking on various public commissions. She was killed at the age of 72 when a fire broke out in her studio.

Hepworth at 47 in her St. Ives studio in Cornwall

PELAGOS
Made in 1946

This smooth wooden sculpture was inspired by a view of the coast. It looks a bit like a shell or the curling lip of a wave. Hepworth said she wanted the strings in the middle to express, 'the tension I felt between myself and the sea, the wind or the hills'.

Sculpture to me is primitive, religious, passionate and magical – always affirmative.

ST. IVES

This is a beach at St. Ives, near Hepworth's home in Cornwall. Many of Hepworth's most famous sculptures were inspired by the landscape.

Each sculpture is made up of huge bronze blocks piled on top of one another. They are over 2.5m (9ft) tall.

THE FAMILY OF MAN (THREE FIGURES FROM)
Made in 1970

These three towering sculptures are part of a group of nine. Each sculpture represents a figure in the different stages of human life, from a young girl to a bride and a bridegroom.

JACKSON POLLOCK

1912-1956

American artist Jackson Pollock shocked the art world with his unusual way of painting. Instead of brushing paint onto his canvas, he dripped, poured and splashed it – earning him the nickname 'Jack the Dripper'.

Born in the west of the USA, Pollock moved to New York to study art at the age of 18. He began to suffer from depression, and started to see a therapist. Therapy helped him understand the meaning of his work.

By the 1940s, Pollock had become very successful. He married a fellow artist and moved to the countryside, where he had more space to paint. But after a few years, Pollock fell into a serious depression. One evening in 1956, he went out driving and was killed in a car crash.

Pollock often worked outside in the open air.

Pollock laid his canvases flat on the floor and dripped paint on them from all directions.

> On the floor I feel more at ease... (I can) literally be in the painting.

Sometimes he swung a paint can with a hole in the bottom of it over his canvas.

I can control the flow of paint; there is no accident.

SIGNING OFF
Pollock often signed his name among the drips of paint. Sometimes, as shown here, he even left hand prints on the canvas.

Rather than using oil paint or acrylic, Pollock used tins of household paint.

This is Pollock's studio in Long Island, New York. Pollock painted his most famous paintings inside.

NUMBER 1A
Painted in 1948
This vast painting, filled with dramatic lines and swirls, seems full of energy. Pollock used the whole force of his body to drip paint over the canvas – a technique which became known as 'action painting'. To him, the act of painting was just as important as the picture itself.

MARK ROTHKO

Russian-born painter Mark Rothko made huge paintings, filled with vast expanses of colours.

Rothko came to the USA with his family when he was ten. He excelled at school, and in 1921, he won a scholarship to study liberal arts at Yale University – one of the top US universities. Discouraged by the atmosphere of wealth rather than learning, he dropped out after two years and moved to New York, where he discovered his love for art.

Rothko's art failed to make much impact until the 1950s, when critics started to notice his work. His paintings became the subjects of exhibitions in America and throughout Europe. Despite his success, Rothko battled with depression. At the age of 66, he killed himself, leaving behind over 800 paintings on canvas and more than 2,500 paintings and drawings on paper.

Rothko in his New York studio in 1964

FAMILY

In this photograph of Rothko's family, taken in around 1909, Mark is the second from the right.

The family name was Rotkovich, but he began to sign his paintings 'Rothko' starting in the early 1940s.

UNTITLED
Painted in 1953
This painting is made up of bright, glowing colours and solid shapes. Although Rothko always avoided explaining the meaning of his work, he wanted his paintings to draw you in and encourage you to contemplate your life and humanity.

The picture below is a wash of flowing shapes. It was made just before Rothko began to develop his most famous style of strong, solid blocks of colour.

There is no such thing as a good painting about nothing.

UNTITLED
Painted in 1948

HEAVE HO
Rothko's paintings were so huge, he had to design a system of pulleys in his studio to move them around.

I wanted to paint both the finite and the infinite.

INDEX

ACKNOWLEDGEMENTS

Cover: Van Gogh's paint tubes © RMN-Grand Palais (Musée d'Orsay) / Droits réservés; Leonardo's flying machine © Model reconstruction of da Vinci's design for an aerial screw (wood, cloth and string), Vinci, Leonardo da (1452-1519) (after) / Private Collection / The Bridgeman Art Library; *Self-portrait with a bandaged ear* by Vincent van Gogh © 2017. Photo Scala Florence/Heritage Images; *Self-portrait as an old man* by Leonardo © Portrait of a Bearded Man, possibly a self-portrait, c.1513 (red chalk on paper), Vinci, Leonardo da (1452-1519) / Biblioteca Reale, Turin, Italy / The Bridgeman Art Library; Claude Monet in his garden at Giverny, France © Mary Evans Picture Library; Claude Monet's glasses © Pair of glasses belonging to Claude Monet (1840-1926) 19th-20th century (photo), French School / Musée Marmottan Monet, Paris, France / Giraudon / The Bridgeman Art Library; *Portrait of John Constable aged 20* by Daniel Gardner © 2017. Namur Archive/Scala, Florence. **Pages 2-3:** *Portrait of a man* by Jan van Eyck © 2017. Copyright The National Gallery, London/Scala, Florence; *Margaret, The Artist's Wife* by Jan van Eyck © Portrait of Margaret van Eyck, 1439 (oil on panel), Eyck, Jan van (c.1390-1441) / Groeningemuseum, Bruges, Belgium / The Bridgeman Art Library; *The Virgin and Child with Chancellor Rolin* by Jan van Eyck © 2017. Photo Scala, Florence; *Annunciation* by Jan van Eyck © 2017. Photo Fine Art Images/Heritage Images/Scala, Florence; *Drawing of an Artist* by Bruegel I © akg-images / Erich Lessing; *Hunters in the snow (Winter)* by Bruegel I © 2017. Photo Austrian Archives/Scala Florence; Photograph of Brussels, Belgium © Bernal Revert / Alamy; *Big Fish Eat Little Fish* by Bruegel I © 2017. Photo Fine Art Images/Heritage Images/Scala, Florence; *The Wedding Dance* by Bruegel I © The Wedding Dance, c.1566 (oil on panel), Bruegel, Pieter the Elder (c.1525-69) / Detroit Institute of Arts, USA / City of Detroit Purchase / The Bridgeman Art Library. **Pages 4-5:** *Self-portrait as an old man* by Leonardo © Portrait of a Bearded Man, possibly a Self-Portrait, c.1513 (red chalk on paper), Vinci, Leonardo da (1452-1519) / Biblioteca Reale, Turin, Italy / The Bridgeman Art Library; Photograph of Vinci, Italy © David Lees/Corbis; Model reconstruction of Leonardo's flying machine © Model reconstruction of da Vinci's design for an aerial screw (wood, cloth and string), Vinci, Leonardo da (1452-1519) (after) / Private Collection / The Bridgeman Art Library; Leonardo's drilling machine drawing © Alinari Archives/CORBIS; Leonardo's bombard drawing © Alinari Archives/CORBIS; *Mona Lisa* by Leonardo © The Gallery Collection/Corbis; *A skull sectioned* by Leonardo © Dennis Hallinan / Alamy; *Lady with an ermine* by Leonardo © 2017. Photo Scala, Florence; *The Last Supper* by Leonardo © 2017. Photo Scala, Florence - courtesy of the Ministero Beni e Att. Culturali. **Pages 6-7:** *Portrait of Michelangelo* by Jacopino del Conte © 2017. Photo Scala, Florence; *The Sistine Chapel Ceiling* by Michelangelo © Michele Falzone / Alamy; *David* by Michelangelo © David, 1501 - 1504 (full relief marble), Buonarroti, Michelangelo (1475-1564) / Galleria dell' Accademia, Venice, Italy / Mondadori Portfolio/Electa/Antonio Quattrone / The Bridgeman Art Library; *Self-portrait* by Raphael © akg-images / Cameraphoto; Photograph of Urbino © DEA / G. SOSIO/De Agostini/Getty Images; *The Garvagh Madonna* by Raphael © 2017. Copyright The National Gallery, London/Scala, Florence; *The School of Athens* by Raphael © 2017. Photo Scala, Florence; *Angel holding a tablet* by Raphael © RMN-Grand Palais / Jacques Quecq d'Henripret. **Pages 8-9:** *Self-portrait* by Titian © 2017. Photo Scala, Florence; Perspective view of Venice © 2017. Photo Scala, Florence; *The Holy Family with a shepherd* by Titian © 2017. Copyright The National Gallery, London/Scala, Florence; *Portrait of Gerolamo (?) Barbarigo* by Titian © Portrait of a Man, c.1512 (oil on canvas), Titian (Tiziano Vecellio) (c.1488-1576) / National Gallery, London, UK / The Bridgeman Art Library; *Drawing of the Portrait of Caravaggio* by Ottavio Leoni © akg-images / Rabatti - Domingie; Photograph of Rome © BL Images Ltd / Alamy; *The Basket of Fruit* by Caravaggio © 2017. Photo Scala, Florence; *Supper at Emmaus* by Caravaggio © 2017. Copyright The National Gallery, London/Scala, Florence. **Pages 10-11:** *The Maids of Honour (Las Meninas)* by Velázquez © 2017. Photo Scala, Florence; *Kitchen scene with the supper in Emmaus* by Velázquez © Kitchen scene or Study for Kitchen Maid with the Supper at Emmaus, 1618-1620, by Diego Velázquez (1599-1660), oil on canvas, 56x104 cm / De Agostini Picture Library / The Bridgeman Art Library; *Pope Innocent X* by Velázquez © akg-images / Album; *Self-portrait with glasses* by Goya © 2017. Photo © Batonne, Musee Bonnat © 2017. Photo Scala, Florence; *The Duchess of Alba* by Goya © akg-images / Album; *The Sleep of Reason Produces Monsters* by Goya © The Sleep of Reason Produces Monsters, plate 43 of 'Los Caprichos', published c.1810 (colour engraving), Goya y Lucientes, Francisco Jose de (1746-1828) / Bibliothèque Nationale, Paris, France / Archives Charmet / The Bridgeman Art Library; *The Third of May 1808 in Madrid: the executions on Principe Pio Hill* by Goya © 2017. Photo Scala, Florence. **Pages 12-13:** *Self-portrait as a young man* by Rembrandt van Rijn © Summerfield Press/CORBIS; *The Night Watch* by Rembrandt van Rijn © 2017. Photo Fine Art Images/Heritage Images/Scala, Florence; *An elephant, a drawing* by Rembrandt van Rijn © The Trustees of the British Museum; Rembrandt's house in Amsterdam © Ian Dagnall / Alamy; Detail from *The Procuress* by Jan Vermeer © Archivart / Alamy; *View of Delft* by Jan Vermeer © 2017. Photo Scala, Florence; *The Artist's Studio* by Jan Vermeer © 2017. Photo Austrian Archives/Scala Florence; Photograph of a street in Delft, the Netherlands © Frans Lemmens/Corbis. **Pages 14-15:** *Portrait of John Constable aged 20* by Daniel Gardner © 2017. Namur Archive/Scala, Florence; *Study of Cumulus Clouds* (Constable's sketchbook) by John Constable © Study of Cumulus Clouds, 1822 (oil on paper laid down on panel), Constable, John (1776-1837) / Yale Center for British Art, Paul Mellon Collection, USA / The Bridgeman Art Library; *The Hay Wain* by John Constable © 2017. Copyright The National Gallery, London/Scala, Florence; *Maria Bicknell, Mrs John Constable* by John Constable © 2017. Photo Josse/Scala, Florence; *Self-portrait* by J.M.W. Turner © 2017. Photo Art Media/Heritage Images/Scala, Florence; *Snow Storm: Steam-Boat off a Harbour's Mouth* (1842) by J.M.W. Turner (1775-1851), Tate, London © Tate, London 2017; *The 'Fighting Temeraire'* by J.M.W. Turner © 2017. Copyright The National Gallery, London/Scala, Florence; *The Channel* (Turner's sketchbook) by J.M.W. Turner © The Channel, c.1845 (graphite & w/c on paper), Turner, Joseph Mallord William (1775-1851) / Yale Center for British Art, Paul Mellon Collection, USA / The Bridgeman Art Library. **Pages 16-17:** Photograph of Édouard Manet aged 38 © akg-images; *Music in the Tuileries Gardens* by Édouard Manet © 2017. Copyright The National Gallery, London/ Scala, Florence; Photograph of Paris, France © Bettmann/CORBIS; *Berthe Morisot with a bouquet of violets* by Édouard Manet © 2017. Gaspart/Scala, Florence; *The Cats' Rendezvous* (poster for an illustrated book on cats by Champfleury) by Édouard Manet © RMN-Grand Palais / Agence Bulloz; Claude Monet's glasses © Pair of glasses belonging to Claude Monet (1840-1926) 19th-20th century (photo), French School / Musée Marmottan Monet, Paris, France / Giraudon / The Bridgeman Art Library; Claude Monet in his garden at Giverny, France © Mary Evans Picture Library; *Caricature of Jules Didier* by Claude Monet © Claude Monet, French, 1840-1926, Caricature of Jules Didier, c. 1858, Charcoal, heightened with white chalk, with smudging, on blue laid paper (discolored to light brown), 616 x 436 mm, The Art Institute of Chicago, IL, USA Mr and Mrs Carter, H. Harrison Collection/Bridgeman Images; *Water-lilies: Morning* by Claude Monet © Waterlilies: Morning, 1914-18 (centre right section), Monet, Claude (1840-1926) / Musée de l'Orangerie, Paris, France / Giraudon / The Bridgeman Art Library; Monet in his studio © Claude Monet (1840-1926) in front of his paintings 'The Waterlilies', in his studio at Giverny, 1920 (gelatin silver print) (b/w photo), Manuel, Henri (1874-1947) / Musée Marmottan Monet, Paris, France / Giraudon / The Bridgeman Art Library; **Pages 18-19:** *Self-portrait* by Edgar Degas © 2017. Image copyright The Metropolitan Museum of Art/Art Resource/Scala, Florence; *The Dancing Lesson* by Edgar Degas © Dancers in the Classroom, c.1880 (oil on canvas), Degas, Edgar (1834-1917) / Sterling & Francine Clark Art Institute, Williamstown, Massachusetts, USA / The Bridgeman Art Library; *Little Dancer aged 14* by Edgar Degas © 2017. DeAgostini Picture Library/Scala, Florence; Edgar Degas' box of pastels © RMN-Grand Palais (Musée d'Orsay) / Hervé Lewandowski; *Dancer adjusting her shoulder strap* by Edgar Degas © BnF, Dist. RMN-Grand Palais / image BnF; Vincent van Gogh's paint tubes © RMN-Grand Palais (Musée d'Orsay) / Droits réservés; *Self-portrait with a Straw Hat* by Vincent van Gogh © 2017. Image copyright The Metropolitan Museum of Art/Art Resource/Scala, Florence; *Self-portrait with a bandaged ear* by Vincent van Gogh © 2017. Photo Scala Florence/Heritage Images; *Starry Night* by Vincent van Gogh © 2017. Digital image, The Museum of Modern Art, New York/Scala, Florence; Vincent van Gogh's letters to his brother, Theo © Van Gogh Museum, Amsterdam (Vincent van Gogh Foundation). **Pages 20-21:** Photograph of Paul Gauguin © akg-images; *The Vision after the Sermon* by Paul Gauguin © 2017. White Images/Scala, Florence; *Arearea* by Paul Gauguin © 2017. A. Dagli Orti/Scala, Florence; Gauguin's sketches in Tahiti © RMN-Grand Palais (Musée d'Orsay) / Hervé Lewandowski; *Coconut sculpted into a face* by Paul Gauguin © Coconut sculpted into a face, c.1895, Gauguin, Paul (1848-1903) / Private Collection / The Bridgeman Art Library; Henri Matisse photograph © REX/LP / Roger-Viollet; Photograph of Collioure, France © Jean-Pierre Lescourret/Corbis; *View of Collioure*, c. 1905 (oil on canvas), Matisse, Henri (1869-1954) / The State Heritage Museum, St. Petersburg, Russia © Succession H. Matisse / DACS 2017, Photograph © The State Hermitage Museum / photo by Vladimir Terebenin; *Sorrow of the King* by Henri Matisse © Succession H. Matisse / DACS 2017, Photograph © akg-images / Erich Lessing; Photograph of Matisse in bed © Condé Nast Archive/Corbis; **Pages 22-23:** *Picasso's Breadrolls*, 1952 © Robert Doisneau/Rapho; *Le Picador* by Pablo Picasso © Succession Picasso/DACS, London 2017, photo credit: © 2017. Photo Art Resource/Scala, Florence; Photograph of *Le Lapin Agile* © akg-images; *Seated Woman (Marie-Thérèse Walters)* by Pablo Picasso © Succession Picasso/DACS, London 2017, photo credit: © 2017. Josse/Scala, Florence; *She-Goat* by Pablo Picasso © Succession Picasso/DACS, London 2017, photo credit: © 2017. Digital image, The Museum of Modern Art, New York/Scala, Florence; *Portrait of Georges Braque* © Portrait of Georges Braque (1882-1963) (b/w photo), French School / Private Collection / Archives Charmet / The Bridgeman Art Library; *Trees at l'Estaque* by Georges Braque © ADAGP, Paris and DACS, London 2017, photo credit: © Trees at l'Estaque, 1908 (oil on canvas), Braque, Georges (1882-1963) / Statens Museum for Kunst, Copenhagen, Denmark / De Agostini Picture Library / The Bridgeman Art Library; *Musical Forms* by Georges Braque © 2017. ADAGP, Paris and DACS, London 2017, photo credit: © 2017, Photo The Philadelphia Museum of Art/Art Resource/Scala, Florence; *Tree of Jesse* by Georges Braque © ADAGP, Paris and DACS, London 2017, photo credit: © Tree of Jesse (stained glass), Braque, Georges (1882-1963) / Collection of Painton Cowen, London, UK / The Bridgeman Art Library. **Pages 24-25:** *René Magritte and the apple* © ADAGP, Paris and DACS, London 2017, photo credit: © 2017. BI, ADAGP, Paris/Scala, Florence; *The Treachery of Images* by René Magritte © ADAGP, Paris and DACS, London 2017, photo credit: © 2017. Digital Image Museum Associates/LACMA/Art Resource NY/Scala, Florence; *The Empire of Lights* by René Magritte © ADAGP, Paris and DACS, London 2017, photo credit: © 2017. BI, ADAGP, Paris/Scala, Florence; Photograph of Salvador Dalí © Twine/ Associated newspapers/REX; *The Persistence of Memory* by Salvador Dalí. © Salvador Dali, Fundació Gala-Salvador Dalí, DACS, 2017, photo credit: © 2017. Digital image, The Museum of Modern Art, New York/Scala, Florence; Photograph of Cadaqués © Roberto Westbrook/SuperStock/Corbis; *Lobster Telephone* by Salvador Dalí © Salvador Dali, Fundació Gala-Salvador Dalí, DACS, 2017, photo credit: Lobster Telephone, 1936 (see also 24815), Dali, Salvador (1904-89) / Ex-Edward James Foundation, Sussex, UK / The Bridgeman Art Library. **Pages 26-27:** *Portrait of Edward Hopper* © John Loengard/Time & Life Pictures/Getty Images; *Automat* by Edward Hopper © 2017. DeAgostini Picture Library/Scala, Florence; Page from Edward Hopper's journal © Edward Hopper (1882 1967). Artist's ledger Book III, (page 27 Seven A.M.). 1924 1967. Pen and ink, graphite pencil, and colored pencil on paper, Book:12 3/16 x 7 5/8 x 3/4in. (31 x 19.4 x 1.9cm). Whitney Museum of American Art, New York; gift of Lloyd Goodrich 96.210 © Heirs of Josephine N. Hopper, licensed by the Whitney Museum of American Art Digital Image © Whitney Museum of American Art; New York Subway Construction Photograph (PR 069, Box 27) on 7th Ave, June 10 1914; image #86451 d, © New York Historical Society; *Early Sunday Morning* by Edward Hopper © Edward Hopper (1882 1967). Early Sunday Morning, (1930). Oil on canvas, 35 3/16 x 60in. (89.4 x 152.4 cm). Whitney Museum of American Art, New York; purchase, with funds from Gertrude Vanderbilt Whitney 31.426 © Whitney Museum of American Art, N.Y.; Portrait of Frida Kahlo © Bettmann/CORBIS; *The Bus* by Frida Kahlo. Banco de México Diego Rivera Frida Kahlo Museums Trust, Mexico, D.F. / DACS 2017, photo credit: © akg-images; *Self-portrait (The Frame)* by Frida Kahlo. Banco de México Diego Rivera Frida Kahlo Museums Trust, Mexico, D.F. / DACS, 2017, photo credit: Centre Pompidou, MNAM-CCI, Dist. RMN-Grand Palais / Jean-Claude Planchet; Photograph of Frida Kahlo and Diego Rivera © Gamma-Keystone via Getty Images; The blue house (Frida Kahlo's house) © John Warburton-Lee Photography / Alamy. **Pages 28-29:** Portrait of Henry Moore and his daughter, Mary © Felix H. Man/Pix Inc./Time Life Pictures/Getty Images; Photograph of Castleford, Yorkshire © The Keasbury-Gordon Photograph Archive / Alamy; *Mask* by Henry Moore © akg-images, Reproduced by permission of the Henry Moore Foundation; *Reclining Figure* by Henry Moore, Photographer: David Mitchinson, Reproduced by permission of the Henry Moore Foundation; Portrait of Barbara Hepworth © Pictorial Press Ltd / Alamy; *Pelagos* (1946) by Barbara Hepworth (1903-1975), Tate, London, © Bowness, photo credit: © Tate London 2017; *The Family of Man* by Barbara Hepworth, © Bowness, photo credit: © foto-zone / Alamy. **Pages 30-31:** Jackson Pollock Photograph by Hans Namuth © Hans Namuth Ltd, courtesy Pollock-Krasner House and Study Center, East Hampton, NY; Number 1A by Jackson Pollock © The Pollock-Krasner Foundation ARS, NY and DACS, London 2017, photo credit: © 2017. Digital image, The Museum of Modern Art, New York/Scala, Florence; Jackson Pollock's paint cans © Susan Wood/Hulton Archive/ Getty Images; Jackson Pollock's studio © Randy Duchaine / Alamy; Mark Rothko photograph © Apic/Hulton Archive/Getty Images; Photograph of the Rothkowitz family, photo - free list © 2005 Kate Rothko Prizel and Christopher Rothko; *Untitled* (1953) by Mark Rothko © 1998 Kate Rothko Prizel & Christopher Rothko ARS, NY and DACS, London, photo credit: Untitled, 1953 (oil on canvas), Rothko, Mark (1903-70) / Private Collection / Photo © Christie's Images / Bridgeman Images; *Untitled* (painted in 1948) by Mark Rothko © 1998 Kate Rothko Prizel & Christopher Rothko ARS, NY and DACS, London, photo credit: © Fondation Beyeler, Riehen/Basel, Beyeler collection.

Additional design by Emily Barden. Digital manipulation by John Russell. With thanks to Ruth King.

This edition first published in 2018 by Usborne Publishing Ltd., Usborne House, 83-85 Saffron Hill, London EC1N 8RT, England. www.usborne.com Copyright © 2018, 2014 Usborne Publishing Ltd. All rights reserved. No part of this publication may be reproduced, stored in a retrieval system or transmitted in any form or by any means, electronic, mechanical, photocopying, recording or otherwise, without the prior permission of the publisher. The name Usborne and the devices ♀♀ are Trade Marks of Usborne Publishing Ltd. UKE.

The websites recommended at Usborne Quicklinks are regularly reviewed but Usborne Publishing is not responsible and does not accept liability for the availability or content of any website other than its own, or for any exposure to harmful, offensive or inaccurate material which may appear on the Web.